30 Days of Prompt

What excuse are you giving yourself right now?

What 3 big adventures would you like to have this month?

What things are so fun to you that you never get tired of doing?

Are you happy with your current way of organising things?

List the distractions you are giving into at the moment?

List all the things you are worried about. will still matter in a year's time.

If you could have an infinite supply of one thing, Why that thing?

Every day, I show my compassion by…

What one act of kindness from a stranger moved you the most?

Would you keep a friend who spoke to you in the way you speak to yourself about you?

What do you want less in your life?

Write all the things that make your body feel nourished.

What is your body saying to you?

What new thing do you want to go and see this week?

What time during the week do you feel most refreshed? What do you do just before it?

What do you know, more than anyone else you know?

Write all the things you associate with the word 'wild'.

What is your 5 greatest strength as a friend?

Is there a space in your home for something you love to do? If not, what can you let go of to make space?

What new projects are lying just underneath the surface? You don't have to do them, just name them.

What positive thing do you bring to your relationship with your family?

List 3 things you could ask others to do instead of doing them yourself?

What one thing could you add to your evening routine that would make a difference to your wellbeing?

In order to create joy, I need…

What or who would make you feel more supported through your brave moments?

What can you do to choose love today?

What does abundance look like to you? Write 20 things that would make you feel abundant.

What guilty thought are you ready to let go of today?

Imagine yourself lit up. Where in your body is the light coming from? Why there?

What were your successes this month?

Made in the USA
Las Vegas, NV
23 April 2024

89049532R00020